Fasting

A Fresh Look at an Old Discipline

David Bolster

Vicar, St Aldhelm's, Edmonton, London

Anna de Lange

Reader and Chaplain to Durham School

GROVE BOOKS LIMITED
RIDLEY HALL RD CAMBRIDGE CB3 9HU

Contents

Acknowledgments

We would like to thank members of the Spirituality group for their encouragement to us to write this booklet. Special thanks are due to Alison Fry, David Runcorn and Philip Seddon for their helpful comments at several stages in the process. Bible quotations are from the *New International Version*.

The Cover Illustration is by Peter Ashton

First Impression November 2002
ISSN 0262-799X
ISBN 1 85174 514 9

Introduction 1

Sometimes it is difficult to know what to do for the best.

We are pulled this way and that between 101 things that impinge on our lives—the national and international news, ecological issues, a friend with cancer, our own worries. In our everyday lives we are encouraged to be crazy consumers. Every street corner has a sweet shop, or a coffee bar, or a take-away. Take a break—eat something. Want to relax? Have a cigar—a whisky—a new car—a tropical holiday. Go on, why don't you? Spoil yourself, you're worth it.

At the same time we live in a culture obsessed by dieting and healthy life-style. The secular idea of 'giving something up' has never been stronger. Diet books abound, for better health as well as for weight loss. We are en-couraged to avoid various foodstuffs for our own good or for the sake of the environment. Hunger strikes are an accepted form of protest, and there are arguments about the ethics of food production that lead to the boycott of certain products. Ramadan is becoming better known and many people are impressed by this fasting element in their Mus-lim colleagues. They admire the strength of character it shows and the dedication to living out religious belief. Christians can look very flabby in comparison.

Nowadays fasting is sidelined as something for 'professionals'

Why are Christians often uptight about over-in-dulgence in alcohol, tobacco, gambling or the cinema, while we neglect our greed for food? We spend a lot of the year giving things up for one reason or another, yet during Lent we either find it difficult to do, or fail to appreciate it because it is simply 'more of the same.'

The Bible and the Church Fathers teach that fasting can be a means of con-centrating the mind, of helping us to think. Yet nowadays fasting is regarded as an oddity—sidelined as something for 'professionals,' or for those with a particular penchant for penitence, mortification of the flesh and self-denial. Why have Christians lost the discipline of fasting? What *is* fasting? Is it the same thing as abstinence or self-denial, or not?

2 What Is Fasting Anyway?

Before going any further you might like to pause and think what 'fasting' means to you.

How many of the following statements describe 'fasting' by your own definition?

1. I'm so worried about my father, I can't eat a thing.
2. I can't justify fattening up animals when so many people are starving, so I'm a vegetarian.
3. He doesn't eat bananas; they make him ill.
4. She only buys fairly-traded teabags.
5. I go to the prayer meeting on Tuesdays, instead of eating lunch.
6. He's given up TV for Lent.
7. My doctor told me not to eat red meat.
8. I can't have my operation till I've lost two stone, so I'm skipping breakfast and lunch.
9. I'm boycotting anything made by X & Co because they use sweat - shops and exploit their workers.
10. We eat fish on Fridays.
11. Will you join the silent witness for peace on Saturday mornings in the High Street?
12. She doesn't eat breakfast until she gets back from church.
13. Not for me, thank you; two glasses is my limit.
14. Thursday is my preparation day, and I don't eat until the children get back from school.
15. Battery farming is cruel, so I buy free-range eggs.

Dictionary definitions of fasting are all very similar, assuming that a person abstains from food (or some food) and maybe drink as well, with the essential element that this abstention should be for religious reasons. It is this last point that differentiates a fast from most slimming diets, food fads, hunger strikes and so on. But there the agreement ends, for there are many different views about what the person fasting should give up and how long that abstinence should continue if the activity is truly to be called 'fasting.' Sometimes the word is modified, so that:

- an *absolute* fast is one in which no food or liquid in any form is taken;
- a *normal* fast might allow liquids, but not the consumption of solid food, for a defined time;
- and a *partial* fast allows some food, though from a limited range.

Therefore while some would describe a fast as being 'nil by mouth' for at least 24 hours, others would say that eating a simple meal rather than one that is normally fuller can constitute a fast. How can we decide to do something if the definitions are this confused? Is there a way through?

The Biblical Tradition

Old Testament
Old Testament spirituality assumed a tradition of fasting, although the precise understanding of what fasting involved varied. It is clear from the stories that the Jews had many different definitions. Esther (Esther 4.16) called for Jews to refrain from eating or drinking anything for three days and nights (this is the maximum time the fit human body can go without fluid without risk to life and health). Daniel and his companions ate only vegetables and drank only water (Daniel 1.12–13). Some fasts were for one day, some for three, some for longer.

The Jewish Calendar had only one obligatory fast, on the Day of Atonement, but there are stories of other fasts which show that from the earliest times fasting was a normal response to certain situations. For example Abraham's servant refused food until he had spoken (Genesis 24.33), David fasted in mourning for Saul and Jonathan (2 Samuel 1.12), the king of Nineveh called on his people to fast and return to God (Jonah 3.6–9), and Daniel fasted as he prayed for his people (Daniel 9.3–4).

New Testament
It is clear that the practice continued into New Testament times. Jesus fasted for 40 days in the wilderness (Matthew 4.2); the disciples of John the Baptist and the Pharisees fasted (Luke 5.33); the apostles fasted (for example Acts 13.2 and 14.23). But we still see a variety of practice and usually it is not clear what the fast involved. Jesus must have taken at least water during his time in the wilderness, and the gospel accounts refer to his hunger when the time came to an end but not to his thirst. On the other hand, Paul neither ate nor drank for three days after his encounter on the road to Damascus (Acts 9.9). Jesus comments on the principle of fasting, but not upon the details of the practice. We should therefore probably assume that he is not advocating an entirely new regime, but expects the Old Testament pattern to continue.

The Historical Perspective

The Early Church Fathers

The early church was accustomed to fasting (according to the *Didache*) on Wednesdays and Fridays. By the late fifth century this had become Fridays and Saturdays as part of the weekly rhythm of three days reflecting the passion, a time of waiting and then the joy of the resurrection.[1]

As well as a weekly fast there were also annual seasons of fasting. By the fourth century the forty days of Lent were being observed as a fast, especially by new believers as part of their preparation for baptism at Easter. In later times other seasons and days were added to the list.

We do not know exactly what this fasting involved. But Tertullian, who became especially interested in the discipline of fasting after becoming a Montanist, describes it as being '...content with a simple diet and pure drink of water.'[2] This is no 'absolute fast.'

Reformation and Puritan England

There is a long tradition that includes abstinence within the definition of a genuine fast. In Reformation England fasting was often interpreted as refraining from eating meat—this was the discipline for Fridays and in Lent. Shrove Tuesday pancakes are the remnant of a tradition that used up the last of the eggs, milk and butter before Ash Wednesday, and marked the beginning of the abstention from all animal-derived produce. In the mid-sixteenth century fasting is described as a reduction to one meal a day in which meat and wine, among other things, should be avoided.[3] It meant a more frugal approach by rich people to the food they ate, combined with giving what would have been eaten to the poor. So we see that the modern tradition of a 'frugal lunch' has a long history, and can properly be included within a definition of 'fasting.'

The modern traditio of a 'frugal lunch' h a long history

Fasting Communion

The waters were somewhat muddied in the nineteenth century by the Oxford Movement's promotion of 'fasting communion' (the practice of not eating until after receiving holy communion) which then came to be regarded as the main form of fasting. This can be a valuable discipline, as long as we see it as one option among many.

The Church Fathers taught that Holy Communion should be the climax of your week, and was not to be taken lightly, so it was important to prepare yourself spiritually and physically. What would be the worst scenario? To come to the worship drunk and so dishonour the celebration of the Lord's Supper. In this situation fasting restores discipline and order. Nowadays of course most of us have a frugal breakfast anyway, and Holy Communion is an early to mid-morning service. Maybe we would think differently if we regularly shared in Communion at 3pm, after Sunday lunch—in our culture one of the largest meals of the week.

Fasting or Abstinence?

Until recent times, fasting and abstinence were interchangeable words. The *Book of Common Prayer* refers to Lent as a time of 'fasting, or abstinence' and, as we have seen, the roots for this go far back into Old Testament times. However, the dominant definition of fasting has come to be that of eating no food (and possibly drinking no liquid) for at least 24 hours. Many evangelical writers from the Puritans onwards have refused to call a 'partial fast' fasting at all. In their eyes anything short of refusing to take solid food at all is not a fast, but 'merely' abstinence. We do not believe that the biblical and historical evidence support either of these standpoints.

We believe that we have lost a lot that would enrich our prayer lives

About fifty years ago, especially in the Roman Catholic Church and in the Church of England, the tradition of fasting was largely lost. Who told us to stop? One reason was that the Second Vatican Council made the Catholic practice of 'fasting communion' non-obligatory. In addition the Puritan definition only allowed an 'absolute' fast to be worthy of the name. Thus a long and varied tradition going back through church history to the Church Fathers was lost to most people in our churches, except for a nod in the right direction in Lent. We believe that we have lost a lot that would enrich our prayer lives as a consequence.

7

3 Why Bother With Fasting?

Quite bluntly, we should fast because we are told to.

This is the first reason. We fast because Jesus fasted and assumed that any-one who wanted to follow him would also fast. He fasted before he started his ministry, and went out into the desert to do so, being alone with God. In Matthew 6 Jesus makes three assumptions about the spiritual behaviour of his followers, and gives guidance on how that behaviour should be ordered. He teaches his disciples:

> *when* you give alms, do it this way;
> *when* you pray, do it this way;
> *when* you fast, do it this way.

These are not things that we can pick and choose to do if we feel like it; they are all equally part of the normal spiritual duty of the Christian. We are to give, to pray and to fast. Look along the shelves of any library or bookshop and you will see large numbers of publications on our stewardship of money and on how to develop our prayer life both as individuals and corporately, but next to nothing on fasting.

The second reason is that fasting can help develop our relationship with God. When we fast we are expressing that God is more important to us at that moment than food. Jesus points to giving, praying and fasting as as-pects of our life that do not necessarily gain us credit on earth, but through which we store up treasure in heaven (Matthew 6.19–29). Where we keep the things that are most precious to us reveals where our heart is. Even Phar-aoh recognized that when he refused to let the Israelites take their possessions out of Egypt (Exodus 10.24–27). We do not necessarily pick up the dividend in this life, though relationship with God is a source of strength when times are bad. So all these are things that we should do privately and without fuss, not making a great show in order to impress the neighbours (Matthew 6.16).

Third, at the very least we can fast because Jesus did. As an observant Jew it seems likely that he kept the major feast and fast days, but the supreme example is his 40-day fast in the wilderness before he embarked on his pub-lic ministry. Many Christians have found that an occasional 'big, one-off' fast can be a major growth point in their lives.

Fasting Without Involving Food

The key is that the intent is spiritual rather than physical—what we fast from should help us to pray and to bring our thoughts closer to God's. Fasting from food can be one way of getting those appetites under control, but we are vulnerable to more than our stomachs. Puritan tradition saw the fast as relating to other 'bodily delights' as well as food, and the Muslim fast over Ramadan includes abstinence from smoking and sexual intercourse in daylight hours.

In the spirit of self-denial we can use fasting to bring our life and our bodily desires under God's control. What might extending a fast outside food look like? Just as a desire to over-eat can be overcome by fasting from eating, so we can:

- fast from using the car, to control our tendency towards laziness;
- fast from busy-ness by taking a Sabbath day (which may or may not be a Sunday) to pray;
- fast from window-shopping to control our desire to be fashionable at all times;
- fast from the distraction of the world by unplugging the telephone while we pray;
- fast from exploiting poorer nations by the choices we make while shopping;
- fast from sexual relations to bring our sex-drive under control;
- fast from playing games on the computer to avoid time-wasting.

Jesus challenged a rich young man to sell all he had and give the money to the poor (Matthew 19.21). He reprimanded James and John (Mark 10.42–43) for wanting power, saying that the ways of the world are not the ways of the follower. He tells his disciples uncompromisingly that they are to deny themselves, take up their cross and follow him (Luke 9.23). Following Jesus means putting him first—before money, before power, before self. It means being different from the world with all its greed and acquisitiveness. Fasting can help us to express that difference. It is a case of 'Who is in control here? Is it God, or is it my natural drives?'

Fasting strengthens self-discipline, it lessens the hold of material things upon us, it shows God we mean business, it lessens the power of habit and it enables us to seek God without distraction.[4]

Fasting and Rhythm

In the early centuries of the church, Easter was the prime baptismal season and a young Christian would first be introduced to fasting in Lent as a discipline to help the preparation for baptism. There was a rhythm to life in which days of celebration and feasting were preceded by a fast day. The *Book of Common Prayer* has sixteen 'Vigils, fasts and days of abstinence' and five other periods or days of fasting. Such a rhythm can be an aid to effective prayer and a powerful weapon in spiritual warfare, calling us back to God and reminding us not to let our love for him grow cold.

Fasting and Feasting

If all this seems very austere, and not much fun at all, be encouraged. Fasting should never be connected with a false strand of asceticism that asserts the idea that the flesh is bad and needs mortification through denying its needs. Our bodies are part of God's glorious creation, to be honoured as temples in which the Holy Spirit may dwell.

Remember too that in Christian tradition Sundays are always feast days. If you have given up chocolate, sugar or puddings for Lent you can still eat the squidgiest chocolate pudding for Sunday lunch with a clear conscience. Just remember that the fact you have indulged might make the discipline harder, because on Monday morning you need to start all over again!

Fasting—But Beware

As with all religious practices, we need to be careful that we do not slip into legalism or self-righteousness. The story of fasting through the centuries has often been one of a slide into formality and tokenism. The absolute fast becomes one which allows water, and then allows other liquids, which soon include rich soups and broths. A fast which allows only vegetables widens to permit dairy produce and then fish, abstaining only from meat. The end purpose of fasting is always spiritual growth, not the abstention in itself.

The end purpose of fasting is always spiritual growth, not the abstention in itsel

Second, there is a danger of hypocrisy. Maybe the development of a relationship with God becomes secondary to demonstrating that we are observant, maybe we adopt special clothes and long faces, or observe the fast in public but break it in private. Jesus is perfectly clear (Matthew 6.16–18) that a fast undertaken with this attitude is worthless. 'When you fast, do not look sombre as the hypocrites do…they have received their reward in full.'

Fasting for...What?

Fasting helps us to get to grips with our need for God, our struggle with self and our concern for others.

We humble ourselves before God, putting him before some other aspect of our life that has been more important. In this new attitude of dependence we can receive guidance (as the apostles did when they appointed Saul and Barnabas, Acts 13.1–3), our faith is encouraged, and our lives, our prayer and our preaching can be empowered anew by the Spirit.

In this chapter we look at six themes from the Bible and tradition that have special connections with fasting.

Fasting and Hunger for God's Word

Perhaps the reason why so often Christians struggle to get spiritually hungry and others do not get spiritually hungry at all is because we are too full. Our lives have so much more built in to them than they did a generation ago. We have work and leisure, relationships and responsibilities, ambitions and plans, all competing for our time and attention. In such a context it is not surprising that few get to a place where they can arrive at church ready and eager to hear God's word—without all those other things either delaying them getting there or clogging the air waves. Put simply, our lives are too full.

Hunger is one of the most basic human drives. We can learn to get to grips with that hunger, to recognize the compulsion to stop what we are doing in order to find food, and to transfer that urge into satisfying the spiritual side of our lives. The most dramatic story of fasting in the gospels is that of Jesus, driven by the Holy Spirit into the wilderness to fast for 40 days, and setting aside family, work and comfort as well as food. Matthew and Luke state baldly that at the end of it 'he was hungry.' He was also clear that he needed to lay aside any ambition for personal success, gain or glory in order to fulfil God's will for his life. It appears that as Jesus grappled with his hunger he used it

Jesus needed to lay aside any ambition for personal success, gain or glory in order to fulfil God's will for his life

to focus on the spiritual hunger which he must never lose sight of in the years to come. 'Man does not live on bread alone, but on every word that comes from the mouth of God' (Matthew 4.4).

In Jesus' ministry we often see him meeting the physical needs of those around him, but also using those needs to draw attention to their spiritual needs. A good example of this lies in John's account of the feeding of the 5,000. First he draws attention to Jesus' observation that the people returned because they had eaten their fill (John 6.26). They missed the sign. Jesus satisfied their physical hunger but especially desired their spiritual hunger. 'Work for food that endures to eternal life' (John 6.27). The physical hunger should have created the spiritual hunger, but it did not. Jesus would have satisfied that spiritual hunger, revealing himself as 'the bread of life' (v 35). When physical hunger creates spiritual hunger then it is to be welcomed.

When physical hunger creates spiritual hunger then it is to be welcomed

How might we do this? One way might be to introduce periods of fasting, or fasting on a Sunday morning, precisely so as to feel the physical hunger, and use it to become spiritually hungry too. The person fasting can use the time, which was originally set aside for eating, to thirst and hunger spiritually, to pray and meditate on God's word.

It is this use of physical hunger to help create spiritual hunger which is behind the tradition of the Lenten fast. One of the oldest spiritual patterns is one of fasting in preparation for a feast to come. For many Christians it lives on in a tradition of abstinence during the forty days before Easter and (to a lesser extent) in Advent.

There is, then, a depth of meaning behind fasting as a physical hungering which directs the Christian to a spiritual hungering, and which can be applied to our lives at any time. Is this why the patristic church used to commend fasting to those preparing to be baptized at Easter?

One of the people the authors interviewed about fasting was Richard. He spoke about the value he has experienced in fasting. 'I am a busy minister. Although I never like to be too busy to pray, I confess that over a period of months I find that my spiritual hunger has disappeared somewhat and I have lost seeking God as God. A short retreat with fasting restores the spiritual hunger quickly.'

Fasting and Penitence

If the answer to the question above is 'Yes,' then it was also for reasons of penitence. The baptized would go down into the water as an expression of their dying to sin. Ash Wednesday opens the Lenten fast with a sharp focus on penitence. It is this meaning of fasting which is perhaps best known today. There is still a tradition (or at least a folk memory), even among people who do not go to church, of eating fish rather than meat in Lent and on Fridays, and possibly fasting completely on Ash Wednesday. Fasting can express 'sorrowfulness of heart' in a way that makes it vivid and real to us.

Each generation of the church has struggled with the problem that a few of those who call themselves Christian, and who may even have been zealous in the recent past, are now going nowhere and are rarely to be seen in church. The even greater problem has been how to receive them back. How can we encourage them to make this a meaningful step and to find a truly repentant heart? Fasting could be a useful part of that process.

Grace is still free but accepting it is not made too easy

One of the difficulties about repentance is finding a way of showing ourselves that we want to be real and honest with God. After all, we know how free his grace is. It was fine when we first became Christians. We were sorry; we may have cried; we meant it; we changed our priorities and sorted out the unrighteous parts of our living. But when all that has been done, how can we get into repentance in a meaningful way? Answer—welcome a penitential fast. Go hungry; welcome the pain of hunger. Then confess. God knows you mean it—but now you also know you mean it! Grace is still free. But accepting it is not made too easy.

We can trace this link back to the Old Testament. There was just one statutory day of fasting in the Hebrew calendar, the Day of Atonement, outlined in Leviticus chapters 16 and 23. On the Day of Atonement God's people came together to recall their sins, and with fasting to declare the sincerity of their sorrow. When the King of Nineveh commands his people to fast (Jonah 3.5) it is an expression of their repentance.

Repentance was a keynote call of both John the Baptist and Jesus, but although neither commends fasting to express outwardly this inner change of heart, the meaning is made obliquely in the parable of the Pharisee and the Tax Collector (Luke 18). The Pharisee voluntarily fasts twice a week, but it is the tax collector who 'merely' breaks down in penitence and is commended for true repentance. Fasting on its own can be completely meaningless. We ought not to misuse this parable to argue that fasting has no place in Christian expressions of penitence. Indeed we have only to look at Matthew 9.14–17 (and parallels). Jesus and his disciples have been criticized for not fasting. Jesus explains why they do not fast, adding that when he is no longer with them, his disciples will then fast.

These verses became a justification for fasting to accompany a remembrance of Jesus' death on Fridays. Friday became the weekly day of atonement, when Christians penitently came to seek forgiveness of their sins as they remembered why Jesus had died. More recently it has been suggested[5] that Jesus is speaking of fasting as an expression of mourning for the death of John the Baptist, and commending a future practice of fasting among his disciples as an expression of mourning for his own death. In that sense a regular Friday fast can help us remember the passion and death that our Saviour suffered because of our sins. This too can be an act of penitence, remembering with sorrow my sin—now forgiven—which led to that awful solution, the passion and cross.

Fasting and Personal Discipline

Discipline has never been easy for any generation—either spiritual discipline or physical. We still teach about having that quiet time and people still find it difficult. When you get to the point of being so fed up with yourself that for the *n*th time your quiet time got squeezed out, and you wonder whether to give up altogether, then it is definitely the time to turn to fasting. Try setting aside one day a week when you will fast at lunchtime and go to a quiet place to pray. When that works, set aside two lunchtimes. When that works, get back to the quiet time. Fasting has done the trick and helped you back into a more disciplined spiritual life, with an established rhythm.

Christians should be able to lead by example since it is our faith which proclaims 'freedom'

When society reaches the levels of freedom, affluence and choice that ours has done, self discipline is important. Christians should be able to lead by example since it is our faith which proclaims 'freedom.' Fasting is a good way of establishing and retaining self-discipline. In 1 Corinthians 9 Paul discusses how he exercises his 'freedom' ('Am I not free?' v 1) and preaches 'strict training' (v 25). He uses an analogy of running a race in which the runner must bring his body under control in order to apply discipline and win.

There are several areas where the Christian should exercise self-discipline— the spending of money, consumption of alcohol, our eating, use of time and personal morality. It is not just the affluence or being bombarded with advertisements, although more discipline is required in a rich society than in a poor one. It is the appeal to our passions. Parents see it most clearly in a young child's plea 'I need!' How difficult it can be to say 'No' to a new shirt which our passion for clothes tells us we 'need' when the cash or plastic is there in the pocket! Have we the will to say 'No' to a third glass of wine, knowing well that two glasses is our personal limit, after which we lose control? The most basic passion of all is food. Our body is so designed that the very smell of cooking or baking introduces gastric fluids into the stomach ready to receive food. Fasting is the means by which we can gain control over this most basic passion.

If we desire the Holy Spirit to have control of our lives then we must let him subdue our basic passions

It is also not just a question of mind over body, but a spiritual matter. If we desire the Holy Spirit to have control of our lives then we must let him subdue our basic passions. Paul states (in Galatians 5.13, 16) 'You were called to be free. But do not use your freedom to indulge the sinful nature…So I say, live by the Spirit, and you will not gratify the desires of the sinful nature.'

When through the help of fasting we have mastered the bodily 'need' for food, we can extend the discipline to other areas of our life which need to come under spiritual control. In that context, to refuse that third glass of wine may have been something which resulted from a spiritual work and is therefore also a 'fast.'

What about physical discipline? The accepted norm is that dieting has nothing to do with fasting, for it is concerned almost exclusively with our obsession with looks and fitness. We want to question that. There are circumstances in which dieting might be a form of fast. The Bible states that our bodies are a 'temple of the Holy Spirit' (1 Corinthians 6.19) and this should lead us to conclude that abusing the body in any way (including over-eating) is wrong. So is loving our neighbour (who might be hungry) less than we love ourselves, by denying him the food that we indulge in. We feel that God does not turn a blind eye to the obese body of a Christian, while being interested in every other aspect of their life.

There are circumstances in which dieting might be a form of fast

Imagine a scenario in which I go to the doctor. The physician says that I am in danger of ill health basically because I am obese. She tells me that I must lose weight and gives me a diet sheet. What she has not done is helped me to look at my attitudes to my diet. Why did I allow myself to become obese? Have I a drive which is even more active than my sex drive? I cannot have my sex drive satisfied on demand (it needs the consent of another) but as soon as I see or smell a food I like, I give way and the waiting is taken out of the wanting. The doctor can tell me what to do, but that does not get to the root of my problem—me, my inability to control my bodily desires and my addiction to food.

Seeing my obesity as a spiritual problem can deal with both the spare tyre and the underlying cause. As well as taking the diet sheet I turn to a spiritual discipline and deliberately fast from one meal, using the time to devote myself to prayer—and in this case penitence as well. I ask the Lord to use the fast to help me take control over my bodily desires. As I gain control, I aim to step up to a 24-hour or even a 36-hour fast. The spiritual aims are various—I may be using the fast to express my hunger for God, or penitence, or even the injustice in the distribution of the food that is such a problem to me, but there is also the bringing of my body under control through the application of the diet sheet. Fasting has done the trick. It has got me into a more disciplined attitude to food.

Greed is not easily recognized by Christians, yet Paul regularly names it as a feature of an unchristian lifestyle (Romans 1.29; Ephesians 5.3, 5; Colossians 3.5; 1 Corinthians 5.10, 11, 6.10). Jesus also labels greed among sins unacceptable for his kingdom (Mark 7.22). The early Church Fathers were often

---

Sarah became obese (24 stone) mostly because of personal hurt and need. She decided to tackle the problem in a holistic way, by strict dieting, healing prayer, spiritual discipline and fasting.

During Lent she fasted from two meals each day, eating only in the evening, while drinking some 8 pints of fluid daily. When she applied fasting to her dieting, she discovered that underlying her habit was a basic passion which she called greed. 'First thing in the morning I'm ravenous, so I now pray during that time.' Even when shopping she would consciously pray when she felt the passion of greed rise within her.

At the end of Lent Sarah had mastered that basic passion and continued her dieting with a lesser fast. Sarah would now not have breakfast until mid-morning, still fasting and praying first thing. She would fast and pray at lunchtime and not eat again until the evening. The result has been that 'I have now mastered the greed. I know when to stop.'

---

concerned with greed among Christians. When indulgence in food and wine preceded worship they were so concerned that fasting was applied as a corrective.

Greed can apply to more than food. It is linked with lust and covetousness in an inter-related trinity of sin which blights the lives of many people (Christian and non-Christian) and even whole cultures. Perhaps we should investigate the levels of greed in various aspects of our lives, and deal with it. It is often more insidiously rooted than we recognize.

Fasting as Self-denial

Closely associated with the understanding of discipline is the emphasis on self-denial. Unfashionable as it may be to take the waiting out of wanting, there is a place for the ancient traditions of the 'desert' in modern spirituality—a place of bareness and simplicity.

Many Christian leaders are urging us in the West to adopt simpler lifestyles, to resist the all-pervasive materialism. Most of us are not called to the monastic self-denial model. We live alongside our neighbours, enjoying many of the privileges which come from our affluence. But surely Christians can also be distinctive in questioning where to draw the line. Should I be content with a more modest house, car, lounge suite, holiday, wardrobe and so on? Surely we can apply the principle of the 'frugal lunch' to other areas of lifestyle.

Surely we can apply the principle of the 'frugal lunch' to other areas of lifestyle

Although today's level of affluence and materialism is new, the issue has been always been relevant for Christians, in the links between abstinence (having less of something) and fasting (doing without it altogether). Abstinence is a form of fasting which focuses on self-denial for a purpose. For example, we might deny ourselves chocolate during Lent. Why? For some it might be merely to demonstrate to themselves and to others that they can be strong willed—but this hardly qualifies it as abstinence for religious reasons. What better motivation might there be? One possibility could be that we are aware that we are lazy about how we spend our money—becoming self-indulgent because the money is there in our pocket. To abstain from chocolate might lead us to a point where we are prepared to sit down and pray through our budgeting. Are we using sufficient of our disposable income for the benefit of others? Do we have the right balance in our lives between luxury and simplicity? Abstinence could be as strong a tool as listening to a sermon about materialism.

Down the centuries Christians have chosen a variety of lifestyles from which to abstain. These fastings have been seen as spiritual rather than physical principles. 'Know that your body is a temple of the Holy Spirit' can be applied to many areas of lifestyle, not just sexual morality.

Paul gives examples of areas of his lifestyle where he has denied himself in order to afford the gospel every opportunity to succeed. He denied himself financial support for his ministry, his limited his Christian freedoms to eat certain meat when with fellow Jews. Jesus promoted this himself: 'If anyone would come after me, he must deny himself and take up his cross daily...' (Luke 9.23) gives us a clue of his standard. His meeting with a rich young man (Matthew 19.16–22) suggests that we need to be wary of the things that control us and replace the reign of God over our lives. Mark 10.29 also has words about self-denial, speaking of those 'who [have] left home or brothers or sisters or mother or father or children or fields for me...'

> *Would-be non-smokers might be helped by fasting. It is well known that it is difficult to give up smoking because it is an addiction. If a period of fasting preceded the date for giving up smoking, the person will have grown in confidence that they can master their own desires, and will be spiritually prepared to break the addiction.*

It is legitimate then, to use fasting in a wider sense than just denial of foods. It can be a corrective against luxury, self-satisfaction, and spiritual laxity.

Fasting to Express Concern for an Issue

We are conditioned in our soundbite culture to hear a plea one minute—even a plea to pray—but to have forgotten it a few hours later. This is not because we are lazy or indifferent but because it competed with other appeals that same day. You must phone this person now. Will you get that work done by the deadline? If we are to protect the call to prayer from the other calls on our lives we need help which fasting can provide. The very fact that I make a decision to drink water but not eat food during the day is a constant reminder to me that today I am praying for the nation, an issue, a situation, a person...maybe using a list of prayer pointers or priorities.

Living in a secular society does not invalidate praying for our nation, for the world and for individual people. There is plenty of biblical precedent, from the King of Nineveh calling a fast of national repentance in response to the preaching of Jonah (Jonah 3) to Mordecai leading the Jewish people to fast in the face of impending holocaust (Esther 4.1–3). The annual Day of Atonement in Leviticus 16 and 23 drew the nation together under God as well as being a time of personal penitence.

f we are to protect the call to prayer from the ther calls on our lives we need help

From the Reformers through to the middle of the 19th Century, the call to the nation for a day of fasting was quite regular, and it was common for either monarch or church to call for a national fast as part of the response to a crisis. For example, there was an outbreak of cholera in 1832, and King William called for 21 March to be a national day of fasting and humiliation on account of the epidemic. The call was even debated in Parliament—was the issue one of public health, or was the outbreak an expression of divine judgment?

More recently there have been calls within sections of the church for a national fast on various occasions, but when the most recent call to prayer was made by the archbishops (following the terrorist attacks on New York and Washington) the call did not explicitly include fasting.

Whereas the idea of a fast on a national scale may seem remote in our post-Christian and postmodern society, there are many in recent times who have included fasting in their concern for one individual. Deeply concerned for a friend we vow to intercede for them in a special time we set aside for the purpose while fasting. This is valuable not just for the individual who is giving priority to this concern in this way but when a group vow together to pray for an individual.

We were told of a church where it was decided to have an evening of prayer for one of the leaders, who was very seriously ill. The invitation to prayer included the suggestion that those who wished to come should prepare themselves by abstaining from food (and drink if they felt able) from lunchtime onwards.

Those who came felt a deeper commitment to the prayer time. And whether by coincidence or not, the symptoms of person they were praying for improved greatly, encouraging the church that fasting was something to be used more frequently.

Fasting for Justice

There is one more strand to fasting which may appeal most to the 21st century Christian, and that is to seek the coming of God's kingdom in justice for all.

Isaiah 58 is a key passage linking fasting with justice. The people ask the prophet why fasting seems not to achieve divine favour (v 3). God responds by pointing out that their fasting does not extend to their actions and their behaviour, for oppression continues and their fasting only serves to make them irritable. Through Isaiah God points out the hypocrisy, the lack of heart-searching, and poses another question: what kind of fast does he desire to see? The answer that God himself gives has nothing to do with the normally-accepted definitions of fasting. Rather, it is that he requires justice for the oppressed, the disenfranchised and the poor. The clear implication is that these attitudes and actions towards our fellow human beings are a form of fasting, with or without abstaining from food. In this context a fast is truly inward, for it is nothing to do with eating or drinking but everything to do with the inclination of our hearts and the expression of those attitudes in our behaviour. We are required to fast from oppression, to fast from injustice, to fast from lack of fairness. Modern calls for the cancellation of debt, or for boycotts of certain goods, or the produce of some countries, for the purchase of fairly-traded coffee, tea, bananas or gifts, can legitimately be included under this definition of a fast.

There is another application of this theme. Up until the 20th century it was established practice among those who fasted to give their meat to the poor, or the money they saved as alms. This tradition has not been entirely lost. Tear Fund have long recommended the 'frugal lunch,' a communal meal accompanied by a talk on issues of justice with an opportunity to give money towards projects of social concern. Many others have adapted the tradition along similar lines. Suggesting that a frugal lunch is not a fast does not do justice to the rich variety of biblical and church practice we looked at above.

> *Young people are often passionate about justice. Why not introduce fasting for justice to the youth programme?*

There is of course no argument against the 'absolute fast.' Indeed, it has much to commend it in our affluent and self-indulgent western society. But it is not the only method of fasting, and as we have seen there are other traditions which have integrity and relevance for liturgy, spirituality and Christian lifestyle.

Rediscovering the Discipline 5

How can we rediscover the self-denial, and even the 'feel-good factor' of doing something so contrary to today's society?

If 'fasting' has a much wider definition and application than is often thought, and if it should be as much a part of our spiritual lives as praying and giving, what does that say about the way we live out our faith in the world today? How and how often might we fast and what might our aims be?

When to Fast?

Fasting is worthless if it becomes a ritual, and should not be 'just' a routine. It is the spirit in which it is carried out that matters, not the frequency. However, just because there are no rules that tell us how often to fast does not mean that we should never do it. We are free to eat and free to fast, as often as we feel inclined or led.

> *A new curate was too tense on Sundays to eat breakfast, and now finds eating before ministering positively unhelpful .*

- Some might feel it appropriate to undertake a regular fast. Sally, married to a non-believer, fasts each Monday from the time she gets up until her husband comes home from work as she prays for him and for other couples she knows in the same situation.

- Others will fast when there is a particular urgency in their prayer. This might be personal or corporate. Biblical examples include the choice of new leaders in Acts 13.1–3 and Acts 14.23.

- Yet others will decide to take the liturgical rhythm of the year more seriously, re-introducing days of preparation and fasting before the feast days, or in times of 'waiting' such as Advent, Holy Week (and especially Good Friday and Holy Saturday) or the days from Ascension Day to Pentecost.

- These days there are other, more recently-introduced, occasions on which fasting might be appropriate. Maybe there are particular groups of people or interests within a church who might be encouraged to fast together: for instance, to remember schools and teachers on Education Sunday, or those who earn their living at sea on Sea Sunday, or farmers and the tourist industry on Rogation Sunday.

- A more personal reason to fast might be the feeling that your own spiritual life lacks discipline. We read in 1 Corinthians 9.27 that Paul pummelled his body in order to be able to concentrate on his calling. If we feel we have grown flabby, that satisfying our bodily desires has become more important than satisfying our spiritual life, then fasting may be a help in redressing that balance.

Decide too how long the fast will last. Some fasts can be quite short but very frequent (such as not eating or drinking until after praying each day) while others might last several days or weeks, but happen less often.

> *One church was called to a day of prayer and fasting when the planning application for an extension to their building was being considered by the local authority.*

What to Fast From?

What sort of a fast might be appropriate? Many find it helpful, like Gilbert and Sullivan, to 'let the punishment fit the crime' and choose a method of fasting that gets directly to grips with the problem. So what choices might be made?

- What is to be given up or abstained from? Will it be food (if so, all food or just one type?) or food and water, or something else that we find compulsive—alcohol, tobacco, video games or shopping?

- Alternatively it could be a fast that involves behaviour rather than food, such as fasting from people (solitude or retreat) that helps us to find space in life to hear God, and to appreciate others for who they are. If you find that your life is dominated by the need for a regular 'news fix,' try abstaining from the media. If your life is dominated by work, take regular 'Sabbath' days when you resolve not only not to do any work, but to turn any of the worries that go round the brain into prayer.

- Fast from answering the telephone, especially if you stop praying to answer it. Let the answering machine take the strain, or just unplug it completely.

- Fast from some habit that makes you so busy that you find you do not have time for God—watching television (are you addicted to one of the soaps?), playing patience on the computer, doing the crossword, whatever it is. But do not lose sight of the fact that God wants us to relax as well as pray!

- Some people find it helpful to treat fasting as doing something positive rather than as 'giving something up.' This could include buying fairly-traded coffee, bananas or chocolate, or setting Sunday lunchtime aside as a time for inviting people we do not know well for a meal, or reading a Lent book (whatever the time of year).

Getting In and Out of a Fast

So what is the best way to start fasting? It is encouraging to experience success, so it is a good idea to have modest aims to start with—maybe missing one meal, or drinking only fruit juice for a day, or cycling to work just once rather than taking the car. Habits can be hard to break, so be realistic and forgive yourself when you lapse.

It is worth knowing that giving up tea and coffee suddenly can give you headaches. It helps if you stop drinking them at least 24 hours before the fast starts, taking plenty of water or fruit juice instead. Many people find it easier to give up food at the beginning of a day rather than at the end once they have already started the day's eating; one person who suffers from migraines triggered by low blood sugar has discovered that she does not get one as long as the fast starts when she gets out of bed. But, for her, breakfast followed by not eating is a recipe for disaster!

Just as it can be helpful to ease your way into a fast, starting to eat again sometimes needs care. If you have only abstained from one meal there is probably no difficulty, but the first solid food after a more extended fast is best if it is fairly light—some fruit, or a salad, or a milky drink. You may find that you have lost the taste for some foods; you can decide whether to reacquire the taste, or to do without them on a longer-term basis.

Never Lose Sight of the Aim

Have a spiritual aim for the fast—what it is you are going to pray for, or how you want to improve your relationship with God—and try not to let yourself be deflected from that aim. At the beginning of your fast make sure the intention is clear to you (writing it down is better still) and return to it at the end of your time. Reflect on what God has taught you, or what you have sensed in a new way, unimpeded by the usual demands of the body. This will be easier if you wait to fast until you have a clear sense that the situation seems right, or even until you feel called by God to fast.

6 A Last Word

*A renewed discipline of fasting could connect with and excite
many people who want to develop their spiritual lives.*

As we have suggested, fasting is much broader than most definitions allow, and can include a wide range of 'abstention,' from more than just food. It is the Godward dimension that separates a fast from merely 'giving up' or dieting.

In this light it is possible to see the fifteen statements of chapter 2 like this.

1. I'm so worried about my father, I can't eat a thing. *Turn the distaste for food into a hunger for prayer for your father.*
2. I can't justify fattening up animals when so many people are starving, so I'm a vegetarian. *Pray for justice in the distribution of the world's wealth and supplies.*
3. He doesn't eat bananas; they make him ill. *Pray for those with dietary illnesses and eating disorders.*
4. She only buys fairly-traded teabags. *Pray for the system that leads to crops being grown for sale abroad rather than to feed the local inhabitants.*
5. I go to the prayer meeting on Tuesdays, instead of eating lunch. *This is a short, conventional (absolute or normal) fast.*
6. He's given up TV for Lent. *Use the time for Bible study, prayer, social action...*
7. My doctor told me not to eat red meat. *Turn the prohibition into prayer for farmers and reflection on modern farming methods.*
8. I can't have my operation till I've lost two stone, so I'm skipping breakfast and lunch. *Pray for control over your drive to overeat, and for others undergoing the same operation.*
9. I'm boycotting anything made by X & Co because they use sweat shops and exploit their workers. *Pray for the system that leads to workers in the under-developed nations being exploited.*
10. We eat fish on Fridays. *Use this as discipline to link yourself with past Christians and their traditions.*
11. Will you join the silent witness for peace on Saturday mornings in

the High Street? *Pray that God will change people's priorities.*
12. She doesn't eat breakfast until she gets back from church. *Pray for a real hunger to meet God.*
13. Not for me, two glasses is my limit. *Pray for all to know what their body can take and for victims of drunken drivers.*
14. Thursday is my preparation day, and I don't eat until the children get back from school. *Use the hunger to teach you to depend on God for the inspiration you need.*
15. Battery farming is cruel, so I buy free-range eggs. *Pray for our stewardship of God's creation.*

Early in his ministry Michael Harper,[6] about to visit the United States and aware that he would find it hard not to over-eat while he was there, went on a diet before he left home. In the course of that diet and his visit he found that:

- he was set free from a craving for food;
- he was fitter and more mentally alert;
- he was more able to cope with temptation;
- he had more concentration in prayer;
- he needed less sleep but felt less tired;
- he was a more effective speaker.

Fasting may affect us, and liberate us from unconscious addictions, in more ways and areas than we initially expect. It can be a reminder to us that all aspects of our lives—physical, emotional, spiritual, moral, intellectual, sensory—are more closely linked than we realize, and that all need bringing under the lordship of Jesus Christ.

Enjoying the Discipline

Fasting does not have to be painful; it can be enjoyable. Jesus tells us (Matthew 6.16–18) not to be miserable about it—and he would not be asking us to be hypocrites. There is a clarity and freshness about a return to basics, to natural conditions and foods. Walk in the park or on the seashore instead of working; eat clean-tasting fruit rather than sweets; drink clear, cool water instead of alcohol. We think of 'just' water in fairly disparaging terms, but in some desert societies a glass of cold, clean water is a gift of real worth, a demonstration of true hospitality to the visitor.

If possible, keep the fact that you are fasting between you and God

If possible, keep the fact that you are fasting between you and God. John, for example, abstains from food for half a day at a time quite regularly, but continues to drink coffee. That way he can go to work and keep up his normal routine, except that he goes for a walk at lunchtime and prays rather than visiting the sandwich bar. One can and should fast and still carry out a normal life, maintaining a spirit of love for God but not necessarily praying every minute of the time. The purpose of fasting is ultimately to open our lives to the Holy Spirit.

A Note of Medical Caution

Going without food (or more especially water) for any length of time can threaten life and health. No-one should embark on even a limited fast without being sure that they are keeping within sensible limits. If in doubt a doctor should be consulted; some medical conditions (for example diabetes, disorders affecting the digestive system, or certain prescribed drugs) mean that regular intake of fluid, food or both is essential. Furthermore, church leaders should never put pressure (practical, moral or spiritual) on an individual to join in a fast. Anorexia and bulimia are never fasting; they are medical conditions requiring expert and long-term treatment.

Further Resources

7

There are overviews of the biblical and patristic traditions in most encyclopaedias and dictionaries of the Bible or the church. Early Christian evidence is discussed in Martin F Connell, *Church and Worship in Fifth-Century Rome: the Letter of Innocent I to Decentius of Gubbio* (Grove/Alcuin Joint Liturgical Studies JLS 52) pp 34ff.

Little has been written from a specifically Anglican viewpoint for over 75 years. Anglican practice is summarized in A J Maclean's chapter 'Fasting and Abstinence' in *Liturgy and Worship* (SPCK, 1932). P Dearmer's, *The Truth about Fasting* (Rivington's, 1928) concentrated on fasting communion.

More Recent Resources

David Smith, *Fasting* (Hodder & Stoughton, 2nd ed, 1974), is comprehensive and discusses all the biblical texts, but unhelpfully discounts abstinence or simplicity as forms of fasting.

Richard J Foster's, *Celebration of Discipline: the Path to Spiritual Growth* (Hodder & Stoughton, 1980) introduced a generation of Christians to fasting.

Elmer Towns, *The Beginner's Guide to Fasting* (Vine Books, 2001) is a practical workbook, although the illustrations all come from the American evangelical scene.

Arthur Wallis, *God's Chosen Fast* (Christian Literature Crusade, 1986) is also commended.

'Fasting reveals the things that control us. We cover up what is inside us with food and other good things, but in fasting these things come to the surface.'[7]

Notes

1   The letter of Innocent I to Decentius of Gubbio. Martin F Connell, *Church and Worship in Fifth-Century Rome: the Letter of Innocent I to Decentius of Gubbio* (Grove/Alcuin Joint Liturgical Studies JLS 52) pp 34ff.

2   Quoted in D Bercot, *A Dictionary of Early Christian Beliefs* (Hendrickson, 1998) p 275.

3   *Book of Homilies*, 1562, 4th homily.

4   Michael Green, *The Message of Matthew* (IVP, 2nd ed, 2000) p 102.

5   For example by C E B Cranfield in his 1963 commentary on Mark's Gospel.

6   Story told in Sr Margaret Magdalen, *A Spiritual Check-up* (Highland Books, 1990) p 83, quoting from US magazine *New Covenant.*

7   Richard Foster, *Freedom of Simplicity* (Triangle, 1981) p 138.